This journal belongs to:

_____

_____

30 DAY Self-Care Challenge

DAY 1	DAY 2	DAY 3	DAY 4	DAY 5
Write in your journal	Pray or meditate	Spend the day social media free	Call someone you love	Take a 15 minute walk outdoors
DAY 6	**DAY 7**	**DAY 8**	**DAY 9**	**DAY 10**
Buy your online cart	Learn to cook a new recipe	Stretch for 10-15 minutes	Listen to your favorite song	Practice deep breathing
DAY 11	**DAY 12**	**DAY 13**	**DAY 14**	**DAY 15**
Try a free online workout	Read a book for 15 minutes	Write a list of short-term goals	De-clutter a room or desk	Go to bed 30 minutes earlier
DAY 16	**DAY 17**	**DAY 18**	**DAY 19**	**DAY 20**
Have a game night	Wake up 15 minutes earlier	Make your favorite meal	Buy yourself something nice	Create a bucket list
DAY 21	**DAY 22**	**DAY 23**	**DAY 24**	**DAY 25**
Watch a movie or series	Write down your thoughts	Take a long shower or bath	Have a home spa day	Eat your favorite snack
DAY 26	**DAY 27**	**DAY 28**	**DAY 29**	**DAY 30**
Create a vision board	Spend some time outside	Get your hair or nails done	Take selfies	Take a power nap

Cupcakes to Myself

I AM:
_____
_____
_____
_____
_____

A LETTER TO MY CURRENT SELF:
_____
_____
_____
_____
_____

A LETTER TO MY FUTURE SELF:
_____
_____
_____
_____
_____
_____
_____

DAILY SELF-CARE

Date ___/___/___
MO TU WE TH FR SA SU

My sleep last night was   Approx. hours _____   Get up time _____

♥♥ ☺ ☹ ☹ 😢

Cups of water 💧 💧 💧 💧 💧   Eye exercises 👁 👁 👁

Day to do list

- Brush teeth and wash face
- Eat breakfast and lunch
- Move my body or take a walk
- Get done work tasks
- Open a window and get fresh air
- Time off screens

Evening to do list

- Read 20 pages of a book
- Write to my journal
- Meditate for 10 minutes
- Workout for 30 minutes
- Brush teeth and wash face
- Take a shower

How I was feeling today

♥♥ ☺ ☹ ☹ 😢

_____
_____
_____

SELF-CARE JOURNALING

Today I felt

Today I needed

Date:

DAILY SELF-CARE

Date _____ / _____ / _____

MO TU WE TH FR SA SU

My sleep last night was   Approx. hours _____   Get up time _____

😍 🙂 😐 😞 😢

Cups of water 💧 💧 💧 💧 💧   Eye exercises 👁 👁 👁

Day to do list

- Brush teeth and wash face
- Eat breakfast and lunch
- Move my body or take a walk
- Get done work tasks
- Open a window and get fresh air
- Time off screens

Evening to do list

- Read 20 pages of a book
- Write to my journal
- Meditate for 10 minutes
- Workout for 30 minutes
- Brush teeth and wash face
- Take a shower

How I was feeling today

😍 🙂 😐 😞 😢

_____
_____
_____

SELF-CARE JOURNALING

Today I felt

Today I needed

Date:

DAILY SELF-CARE

Date ___/___/___

MO TU WE TH FR SA SU

My sleep last night was   Approx. hours _____   Get up time _____

♥︎ ☺ ☹ ☹ ☹

Cups of water 💧 💧 💧 💧 💧   Eye exercises 👁 👁 👁

Day to do list

- Brush teeth and wash face
- Eat breakfast and lunch
- Move my body or take a walk
- Get done work tasks
- Open a window and get fresh air
- Time off screens

Evening to do list

- Read 20 pages of a book
- Write to my journal
- Meditate for 10 minutes
- Workout for 30 minutes
- Brush teeth and wash face
- Take a shower

How I was feeling today

♥︎ ☺ ☹ ☹ ☹

_____
_____
_____

SELF-CARE JOURNALING

Today I felt

_____
_____
_____

Today I needed

_____
_____
_____

Date:

DAILY SELF-CARE

Date ___/___/___

MO TU WE TH FR SA SU

My sleep last night was

Approx. hours _____

Get up time _____

Cups of water 💧 💧 💧 💧 💧

Eye exercises 👁 👁 👁

Day to do list

- Brush teeth and wash face
- Eat breakfast and lunch
- Move my body or take a walk
- Get done work tasks
- Open a window and get fresh air
- Time off screens

Evening to do list

- Read 20 pages of a book
- Write to my journal
- Meditate for 10 minutes
- Workout for 30 minutes
- Brush teeth and wash face
- Take a shower

How I was feeling today

_____
_____
_____

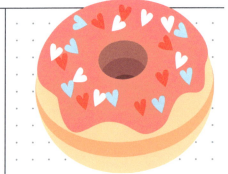

SELF-CARE JOURNALING

| Today I felt | Today I needed |

_____   _____
_____   _____
_____   _____

Date:

DAILY SELF-CARE

Date ____/____/____

MO TU WE TH FR SA SU

My sleep last night was   Approx. hours _____   Get up time _____

♥‿♥ ‿ ‿ ✕✕ ;(

Cups of water 💧 💧 💧 💧 💧   Eye exercises 👁 👁 👁

Day to do list

- Brush teeth and wash face
- Eat breakfast and lunch
- Move my body or take a walk
- Get done work tasks
- Open a window and get fresh air
- Time off screens

Evening to do list

- Read 20 pages of a book
- Write to my journal
- Meditate for 10 minutes
- Workout for 30 minutes
- Brush teeth and wash face
- Take a shower

How I was feeling today

♥‿♥ ‿ ‿ ✕✕ ;(

_____
_____
_____

SELF-CARE JOURNALING

| Today I felt | Today I needed |

Date:

DAILY SELF-CARE

Date ___ / ___ / ___

MO TU WE TH FR SA SU

My sleep last night was

♥♥ ☺ ☹ ☹ 😢

Approx. hours _____

Get up time _____

Cups of water 💧 💧 💧 💧 💧

Eye exercises 👁 👁 👁

Day to do list

- Brush teeth and wash face
- Eat breakfast and lunch
- Move my body or take a walk
- Get done work tasks
- Open a window and get fresh air
- Time off screens

Evening to do list

- Read 20 pages of a book
- Write to my journal
- Meditate for 10 minutes
- Workout for 30 minutes
- Brush teeth and wash face
- Take a shower

How I was feeling today

♥♥ ☺ ☹ ☹ 😢

_____
_____
_____

SELF-CARE JOURNALING

| Today I felt | Today I needed |

_____
_____
_____

Date:

DAILY SELF-CARE

Date ___/___/___

MO TU WE TH FR SA SU

My sleep last night was

♥♥ ☺ 😐 😕 😢

Approx. hours _____

Get up time _____

Cups of water 💧 💧 💧 💧 💧

Eye exercises 👁 👁 👁

Day to do list

- Brush teeth and wash face
- Eat breakfast and lunch
- Move my body or take a walk
- Get done work tasks
- Open a window and get fresh air
- Time off screens

Evening to do list

- Read 20 pages of a book
- Write to my journal
- Meditate for 10 minutes
- Workout for 30 minutes
- Brush teeth and wash face
- Take a shower

How I was feeling today

♥♥ ☺ 😐 😕 😢

_____
_____
_____
_____

SELF-CARE JOURNALING

Today I felt

_____
_____
_____

Today I needed

_____
_____
_____

Date:

Date
____ / ____ / ____
MO TU WE TH FR SA SU

My sleep last night was   Approx. hours _____   Get up time _____

♥♥ ☺ ☹ ☓ ☹

Cups of water 💧 💧 💧 💧 💧   Eye exercises 👁 👁 👁

Day to do list

- Brush teeth and wash face
- Eat breakfast and lunch
- Move my body or take a walk
- Get done work tasks
- Open a window and get fresh air
- Time off screens

Evening to do list

- Read 20 pages of a book
- Write to my journal
- Meditate for 10 minutes
- Workout for 30 minutes
- Brush teeth and wash face
- Take a shower

How I was feeling today

♥♥ ☺ ☹ ☓ ☹

_____
_____
_____

SELF-CARE JOURNALING

Today I felt
_____
_____
_____

Today I needed
_____
_____
_____

Date:

DAILY SELF-CARE

Date ___ / ___ / ___

MO TU WE TH FR SA SU

My sleep last night was   Approx. hours _____   Get up time _____

♥‿♥ ‿ :| >_< ;_;

Cups of water 💧 💧 💧 💧 💧   Eye exercises 👁 👁 👁

Day to do list

- Brush teeth and wash face
- Move my body or take a walk
- Get done work tasks
- Open a window and get fresh air
- Time off screens

Evening to do list

- Read 20 pages of a book
- Write to my journal
- Meditate for 10 minutes
- Workout for 30 minutes
- Brush teeth and wash face
- Take a shower

How I was feeling today

♥‿♥ ‿ :| >_< ;_;

_____
_____
_____
_____

SELF-CARE JOURNALING

Today I felt

_____
_____
_____

Today I needed

_____
_____
_____

Date:

DAILY SELF-CARE

Date ___ / ___ / ___
MO TU WE TH FR SA SU

My sleep last night was

Approx. hours _____   Get up time _____

Cups of water   💧 💧 💧 💧 💧

Eye exercises   👁 👁 👁

Day to do list

- Brush teeth and wash face
- Eat breakfast and lunch
- Move my body or take a walk
- Get done work tasks
- Open a window and get fresh air
- Time off screens

Evening to do list

- Read 20 pages of a book
- Write to my journal
- Meditate for 10 minutes
- Workout for 30 minutes
- Brush teeth and wash face
- Take a shower

How I was feeling today

_____
_____
_____
_____

SELF-CARE JOURNALING

Today I felt

_____
_____
_____

Today I needed

_____
_____
_____

Date:

DAILY SELF-CARE

Date ___ / ___ / ___

MO TU WE TH FR SA SU

My sleep last night was

♥♥ ☺ ☐ ☹ 😢

Approx. hours _____   Get up time _____

Cups of water ○ ○ ○ ○ ○

Eye exercises ◉ ◉ ◉

Day to do list

- Brush teeth and wash face
- Eat breakfast and lunch
- Move my body or take a walk
- Get done work tasks
- Open a window and get fresh air
- Time off screens

Evening to do list

- Read 20 pages of a book
- Write to my journal
- Meditate for 10 minutes
- Workout for 30 minutes
- Brush teeth and wash face
- Take a shower

How I was feeling today

♥♥ ☺ ☐ ☹ 😢

_____
_____
_____

SELF-CARE JOURNALING

Today I felt
_____
_____
_____

Today I needed
_____
_____
_____

Date:

DAILY SELF-CARE

Date ___ / ___ / ___

MO TU WE TH FR SA SU

My sleep last night was   Approx. hours _____   Get up time _____

♥♥ ☺ ☺ ☹ ☹

Cups of water 💧 💧 💧 💧 💧   Eye exercises 👁 👁 👁

Day to do list

- Brush teeth and wash face
- Eat breakfast and lunch
- Move my body or take a walk
- Get done work tasks
- Open a window and get fresh air
- Time off screens

Evening to do list

- Read 20 pages of a book
- Write to my journal
- Meditate for 10 minutes
- Workout for 30 minutes
- Brush teeth and wash face
- Take a shower

How I was feeling today

♥♥ ☺ ☺ ☹ ☹

_____
_____
_____
_____

SELF-CARE JOURNALING

| Today I felt | Today I needed |

_____   _____
_____   _____
_____   _____

Date:
_____
_____
_____
_____
_____
_____
_____
_____
_____
_____
_____
_____
_____
_____
_____

DAILY SELF-CARE

Date ___ / ___ / ___

MO TU WE TH FR SA SU

My sleep last night was   Approx. hours _____   Get up time _____

♥♥ ☺ :| ☹ 😢

Cups of water 💧 💧 💧 💧 💧   Eye exercises 👁 👁 👁

Day to do list

- Brush teeth and wash face
- Eat breakfast and lunch
- Move my body or take a walk
- Get done work tasks
- Open a window and get fresh air
- Time off screens

Evening to do list

- Read 20 pages of a book
- Write to my journal
- Meditate for 10 minutes
- Workout for 30 minutes
- Brush teeth and wash face
- Take a shower

How I was feeling today

♥♥ ☺ :| ☹ 😢

_____
_____
_____

SELF-CARE JOURNALING

| Today I felt | Today I needed |

Date:

DAILY SELF-CARE

Date ___ / ___ / ___
MO TU WE TH FR SA SU

My sleep last night was   Approx. hours _____   Get up time _____

♥‿♥   ◡‿◡   •‿•   ×‿×   ⇀‿↼

Cups of water 💧 💧 💧 💧 💧   Eye exercises 👁 👁 👁

Day to do list

- Brush teeth and wash face
- Eat breakfast and lunch
- Move my body or take a walk
- Get done work tasks
- Open a window and get fresh air
- Time off screens

Evening to do list

- Read 20 pages of a book
- Write to my journal
- Meditate for 10 minutes
- Workout for 30 minutes
- Brush teeth and wash face
- Take a shower

How I was feeling today

♥‿♥   ◡‿◡   •‿•   ×‿×   ⇀‿↼

_____
_____
_____

SELF-CARE JOURNALING

Today I felt
_____
_____
_____

Today I needed
_____
_____
_____

Date:

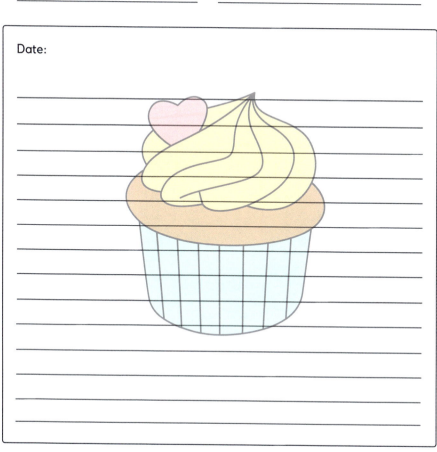

DAILY SELF-CARE

Date ___ / ___ / ___

MO TU WE TH FR SA SU

My sleep last night was ♥♥ ☺ 😐 ☹ 😣

Approx. hours _____

Get up time _____

Cups of water 💧 💧 💧 💧 💧

Eye exercises 👁 👁 👁

Day to do list

- Brush teeth and wash face
- Eat breakfast and lunch
- Move my body or take a walk
- Get done work tasks
- Open a window and get fresh air
- Time off screens

Evening to do list

- Read 20 pages of a book
- Write to my journal
- Meditate for 10 minutes
- Workout for 30 minutes
- Brush teeth and wash face
- Take a shower

How I was feeling today ♥♥ ☺ 😐 ☹ 😣

_____
_____
_____

SELF-CARE JOURNALING

Today I felt

_____
_____
_____

Today I needed

_____
_____
_____

Date:

DAILY SELF-CARE

Date ____/____/____

MO TU WE TH FR SA SU

My sleep last night was ♥♥ ☺ 😐 ☹ 😢

Approx. hours _____

Get up time _____

Cups of water 💧 💧 💧 💧 💧

Eye exercises 👁 👁 👁

Day to do list

- Brush teeth and wash face
- Eat breakfast and lunch
- Move my body or take a walk
- Get done work tasks
- Open a window and get fresh air
- Time off screens

Evening to do list

- Read 20 pages of a book
- Write to my journal
- Meditate for 10 minutes
- Workout for 30 minutes
- Brush teeth and wash face
- Take a shower

How I was feeling today

♥♥ ☺ 😐 ☹ 😢

_____
_____
_____

SELF-CARE JOURNALING

Today I felt

_____
_____
_____

Today I needed

_____
_____
_____

Date:

DAILY SELF-CARE

Date ___/___/___
MO TU WE TH FR SA SU

My sleep last night was
♥♥ ☺ ☹ ☹ 😢

Approx. hours _____

Get up time _____

Cups of water 💧 💧 💧 💧 💧

Eye exercises 👁 👁 👁

Day to do list

- Wash face
- Eat breakfast and lunch
- Move my body or take a walk
- Get done work tasks
- Open a window and get fresh air
- Time off screens

Evening to do list

- Read 20 pages of a book
- Write to my journal
- Meditate for 10 minutes
- Workout for 30 minutes
- Brush teeth and wash face
- Take a shower

How I was feeling today

♥♥ ☺ ☹ ☹ 😢

_____
_____
_____

SELF-CARE JOURNALING

Today I felt

_____
_____
_____

Today I needed

_____
_____
_____

Date:

DAILY SELF-CARE

Date ___/___/___
MO TU WE TH FR SA SU

My sleep last night was   Approx. hours _____   Get up time _____

♥‿♥ ◡ ‿ ︵ ︵'

Cups of water   💧 💧 💧 💧 💧   Eye exercises 👁 👁 👁

Day to do list

- Brush teeth and wash face
- Eat breakfast and lunch
- Move my body or take a walk
- Get done work tasks
- Open a window and get fresh air
- Time off screens

Evening to do list

- Read 20 pages of a book
- Write to my journal
- Meditate for 10 minutes
- Workout for 30 minutes
- Brush teeth and wash face
- Take a shower

How I was feeling today

♥‿♥ ◡ ‿ ︵ ︵'

_____
_____
_____

SELF-CARE JOURNALING

Today I felt

Today I needed

Date:

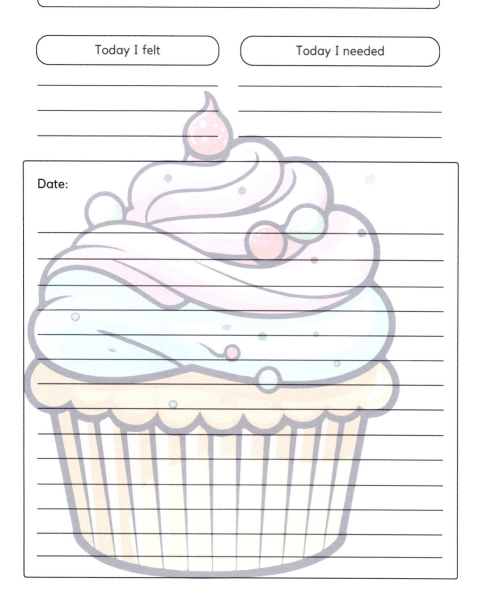

DAILY SELF-CARE

Date ___ / ___ / ___

MO TU WE TH FR SA SU

My sleep last night was

Approx. hours _____   Get up time _____

Cups of water 💧 💧 💧 💧 💧   Eye exercises 👁 👁 👁

Day to do list

- Brush teeth and wash face
- Eat breakfast and lunch
- Move my body or take a walk
- Get done work tasks
- Open a window and get fresh air
- Time off screens

Evening to do list

- Read 20 pages of a book
- Write to my journal
- Meditate for 10 minutes
- Workout for 30 minutes
- Brush teeth and wash face
- Take a shower

How I was feeling today

_____
_____
_____

SELF-CARE JOURNALING

Today I felt

_____
_____
_____

Today I needed

_____
_____
_____

Date:

DAILY SELF-CARE

Date ___/___/___

MO TU WE TH FR SA SU

My sleep last night was   Approx. hours _____   Get up time _____

♥♥ ☺ :|):):•

Cups of water 💧 💧 💧 💧 💧   Eye exercises 👁 👁 👁

Day to do list

- Brush teeth and wash face
- Eat breakfast and lunch
- Move my body or take a walk
- Get done work tasks
- Open a window and get fresh air
- Time off screens

Evening to do list

- Read 20 pages of a book
- Write to my journal
- Meditate for 10 minutes
- Workout for 30 minutes
- Brush teeth and wash face
- Take a shower

How I was feeling today

♥♥ ☺ :|):):•

_____
_____
_____

SELF-CARE JOURNALING

Today I felt

_____
_____
_____

Today I needed

_____
_____
_____

Date:

DAILY SELF-CARE

Date _____ / _____ / _____

MO TU WE TH FR SA SU

My sleep last night was

♥‿♥   ☺   :| ><   :'(

Approx. hours _____

Get up time _____

Cups of water 💧 💧 💧 💧 💧

Eye exercises 👁 👁 👁

Day to do list

- Brush teeth and wash face
- Eat breakfast and lunch
- Move my body or take a walk
- Get done work tasks
- Open a window and get fresh air
- Time off screens

Evening to do list

- Read 20 pages of a book
- Write to my journal
- Meditate for 10 minutes
- Workout for 30 minutes
- Brush teeth and wash face
- Take a shower

How I was feeling today

♥‿♥   ☺   :| ><   :'(

_____
_____
_____

SELF-CARE JOURNALING

Today I felt

_____
_____
_____

Today I needed

_____
_____
_____

Date:

DAILY SELF-CARE

Date ____/____/____
MO TU WE TH FR SA SU

My sleep last night was   Approx. hours _____   Get up time _____
♥‿♥ ‿ ‿ ⁀ ⁀

Cups of water 💧 💧 💧 💧 💧   Eye exercises 👁 👁 👁

Day to do list

- Brush teeth and wash face
- Eat breakfast and lunch
- Move my body or take a walk
- Get done work tasks
- Open a window and get fresh air
- Time off screens

Evening to do list

- Read 20 pages of a book
- Write to my journal
- Meditate for 10 minutes
- Workout for 30 minutes
- Brush teeth and wash face
- Take a shower

How I was feeling today
♥‿♥ ‿ ‿ ⁀ ⁀

_____
_____
_____

SELF-CARE JOURNALING

Today I felt

Today I needed

Date:

DAILY SELF-CARE

Date ___ / ___ / ___

MO TU WE TH FR SA SU

My sleep last night was

♥♥ ☺ :| :(:,(

Approx. hours _____

Get up time _____

Cups of water 💧 💧 💧 💧

Eye exercises 👁 👁 👁

Day to do list

- Brush teeth and wash face
- Eat breakfast and lunch
- Move my body or take a walk
- Get done work tasks
- Open a window and get fresh air
- Time off screens

Evening to do list

- Read 20 pages of a book
- Write to my journal
- Meditate for 10 minutes
- Workout for 30 minutes
- Brush teeth and wash face
- Take a shower

How I was feeling today

♥♥ ☺ :| :(:,(

_____
_____
_____

SELF-CARE JOURNALING

| Today I felt | Today I needed |

_____
_____
_____

Date:

DAILY SELF-CARE

Date ___/___/___

MO TU WE TH FR SA SU

My sleep last night was

♥♥ ☺ 😐 ☹ 😢

Approx. hours _____

Get up time _____

Cups of water 💧 💧 💧 💧 💧

Eye exercises 👁 👁 👁

Day to do list

- Brush teeth and wash face
- Eat breakfast and lunch
- Move my body or take a walk
- Get done work tasks
- Open a window and get fresh air
- Time off screens

Evening to do list

- Read 20 pages of a book
- Write to my journal
- Meditate for 10 minutes
- Workout for 30 minutes
- Brush teeth and wash face
- Take a shower

How I was feeling today

♥♥ ☺ 😐 ☹ 😢

_____
_____
_____

SELF-CARE JOURNALING

Today I felt

_____

_____

_____

Today I needed

_____

_____

_____

Date:

_____
_____
_____
_____
_____
_____
_____
_____
_____
_____
_____
_____
_____

DAILY SELF-CARE

Date ____ / ____ / ____

MO TU WE TH FR SA SU

My sleep last night was   Approx. hours _____   Get up time _____

♥♥   ☺   😐   ☹   😢

Cups of water 💧 💧 💧 💧 💧   Eye exercises 👁 👁 👁

Day to do list

- Brush teeth and wash face
- Eat breakfast and lunch
- Move my body or take a walk
- Get done work tasks
- Open a window and get fresh air
- Time off screens

Evening to do list

- Read 20 pages of a book
- Write to my journal
- Meditate for 10 minutes
- Workout for 30 minutes
- Brush teeth and wash face
- Take a shower

How I was feeling today

♥♥   ☺   😐   ☹   😢

_____
_____
_____

SELF-CARE JOURNALING

Today I felt

_____
_____
_____

Today I needed

_____
_____
_____

Date:

DAILY SELF-CARE

Date ___/___/___

MO TU WE TH FR SA SU

My sleep last night was   Approx. hours _____   Get up time _____

Cups of water 💧 💧 💧 💧 💧   Eye exercises 👁 👁 👁

Day to do list

- Brush teeth and wash face
- Eat breakfast and lunch
- Move my body or take a walk
- Get done work tasks
- Open a window and get fresh air
- Time off screens

Evening to do list

- Read 20 pages of a book
- Write to my journal
- Meditate for 10 minutes
- Workout for 30 minutes
- Brush teeth and wash face
- Take a shower

How I was feeling today

_____
_____
_____

SELF-CARE JOURNALING

Today I felt

Today I needed

Date:

DAILY SELF-CARE

Date ___/___/___
MO TU WE TH FR SA SU

My sleep last night was
♥‿♥   ☺   😐   ☹   😢

Approx. hours _____

Get up time _____

Cups of water 💧 💧 💧 💧 💧

Eye exercises 👁 👁 👁

Day to do list

- Brush teeth and wash face
- Eat breakfast and lunch
- Move my body or take a walk
- Get done work tasks
- Open a window and get fresh air
- Time off screens

Evening to do list

- Read 20 pages of a book
- Write to my journal
- Meditate for 10 minutes
- Workout for 30 minutes
- Brush teeth and wash face
- Take a shower

How I was feeling today

♥‿♥   ☺   😐   ☹   😢

_____
_____
_____

SELF-CARE JOURNALING

Today I felt

_____
_____
_____

Today I needed

_____
_____
_____

Date:

DAILY SELF-CARE

Date ___ / ___ / ___
MO TU WE TH FR SA SU

My sleep last night was

Approx. hours _____   Get up time _____

Cups of water   Eye exercises

Day to do list

- Brush teeth and wash face
- Eat breakfast and lunch
- Move my body or take a walk
- Get done work tasks
- Open a window and get fresh air
- Time off screens

Evening to do list

- Read 20 pages of a book
- Write to my journal
- Meditate for 10 minutes
- Workout for 30 minutes
- Brush teeth and wash face
- Take a shower

How I was feeling today

_____
_____
_____

SELF-CARE JOURNALING

Today I felt

_____

_____

_____

Today I needed

_____

_____

_____

Date:

DAILY SELF-CARE

Date ___ / ___ / ___
MO TU WE TH FR SA SU

My sleep last night was   Approx. hours _____   Get up time _____

♥‿♥ :) :| >_< ;_;

Cups of water 💧 💧 💧 💧   Eye exercises 👁 👁 👁

Day to do list

- Brush teeth and wash face
- Eat breakfast and lunch
- Move my body or take a walk
- Get done work tasks
- Open a window and get fresh air
- Time off screens

Evening to do list

- Read 20 pages of a book
- Write to my journal
- Meditate for 10 minutes
- Workout for 30 minutes
- Brush teeth and wash face
- Take a shower

How I was feeling today

♥‿♥ :) :| >_< ;_;

_____
_____
_____

SELF-CARE JOURNALING

Today I felt

_____
_____
_____

Today I needed

_____
_____
_____

Date:

DAILY SELF-CARE

Date ___/___/___

MO TU WE TH FR SA SU

My sleep last night was   Approx. hours _____   Get up time _____

♥♥ ☺ 😐 ☹ 😢

Cups of water 💧 💧 💧 💧 💧   Eye exercises 👁 👁 👁

Day to do list

- Brush teeth and wash face
- Eat breakfast and lunch
- Move my body or take a walk
- Get done work tasks
- Open a window and get fresh air
- Time off screens

Evening to do list

- Read 20 pages of a book
- Write to my journal
- Meditate for 10 minutes
- Workout for 30 minutes
- Brush teeth and wash face
- Take a shower

How I was feeling today

♥♥ ☺ 😐 ☹ 😢

_____
_____
_____
_____

SELF-CARE JOURNALING

| Today I felt | Today I needed |

_____   _____
_____   _____
_____   _____

Date:

DAILY SELF-CARE

Date ____ / ____ / ____

MO TU WE TH FR SA SU

My sleep last night was

Approx. hours _____   Get up time _____

Cups of water 💧 💧 💧 💧 💧   Eye exercises 👁 👁 👁

Day to do list

- Brush teeth and wash face
- Eat breakfast and lunch
- Move my body or take a walk
- Get done work tasks
- Open a window and get fresh air
- Time off screens

Evening to do list

- Read 20 pages of a book
- Write to my journal
- Meditate for 10 minutes
- Workout for 30 minutes
- Brush teeth and wash face
- Take a shower

How I was feeling today

_____
_____
_____
_____

SELF-CARE JOURNALING

Today I felt

_____

_____

_____

Today I needed

_____

_____

_____

Date:

_____
_____
_____
_____
_____
_____
_____
_____
_____
_____
_____
_____
_____

i am   **DATE**   /   /

i am

DATE   /   /

i am   DATE   /   /

i am   DATE   /   /

daily journal   DATE   /   /

daily journal   DATE   /   /

daily journal   DATE   /   /

daily journal   DATE   /   /

daily journal DATE   /   /

daily journal DATE / /

I am Grateful   DATE   /   /

I am Grateful

DATE   /   /

I am Grateful — DATE   /   /

I am Grateful

DATE   /   /

daily journal DATE   /   /

daily journal   DATE   /   /

daily journal DATE   /   /

daily journal　　　DATE 　　/　　/

daily journal DATE   /   /

daily journal DATE   /   /

daily journal   DATE   /   /

daily journal   DATE   /   /

daily journal   DATE   /   /

daily journal   DATE   /   /

daily journal   DATE   /   /

daily journal   DATE   /   /

daily journal   DATE   /   /

daily journal   DATE   /   /

daily journal		DATE / /

daily journal DATE   /   /

daily journal   DATE   /   /

daily journal   DATE   /   /

daily journal   DATE   /   /

daily journal DATE   /   /

daily journal DATE   /   /

Made in the USA
Columbia, SC
21 March 2025